BILL GILLHAM

The
Early Words
Picture
Book

Photographs by Sam Grainger

CENTENARY HEALTH CENTRE
SPEECH-LANGUAGE PATHOLOGY SERVICES

A Magnet Book

rabbit

Jenny is giving the rabbit a carrot.

bicycle

David is learning to ride his bicycle;
Mummy pulls him along.

bananas

The children are eating bananas.

swing

Jenny likes playing on the swing;
up and down she goes.

duck

The children feed the ducks in the park.

boat

Daddy takes everyone out in a boat.

bubbles

Jenny is blowing bubbles.

doll

David gives the doll a ride in his pushchair.

hat

Jenny is dressing up;
she puts on a pretty pink hat.

tree

Jenny swings in a tyre
that's hanging from the tree.

keys

Baby plays with Mummy's keys;
he shakes and jingles them.

cat

The cat likes Jenny to brush him.

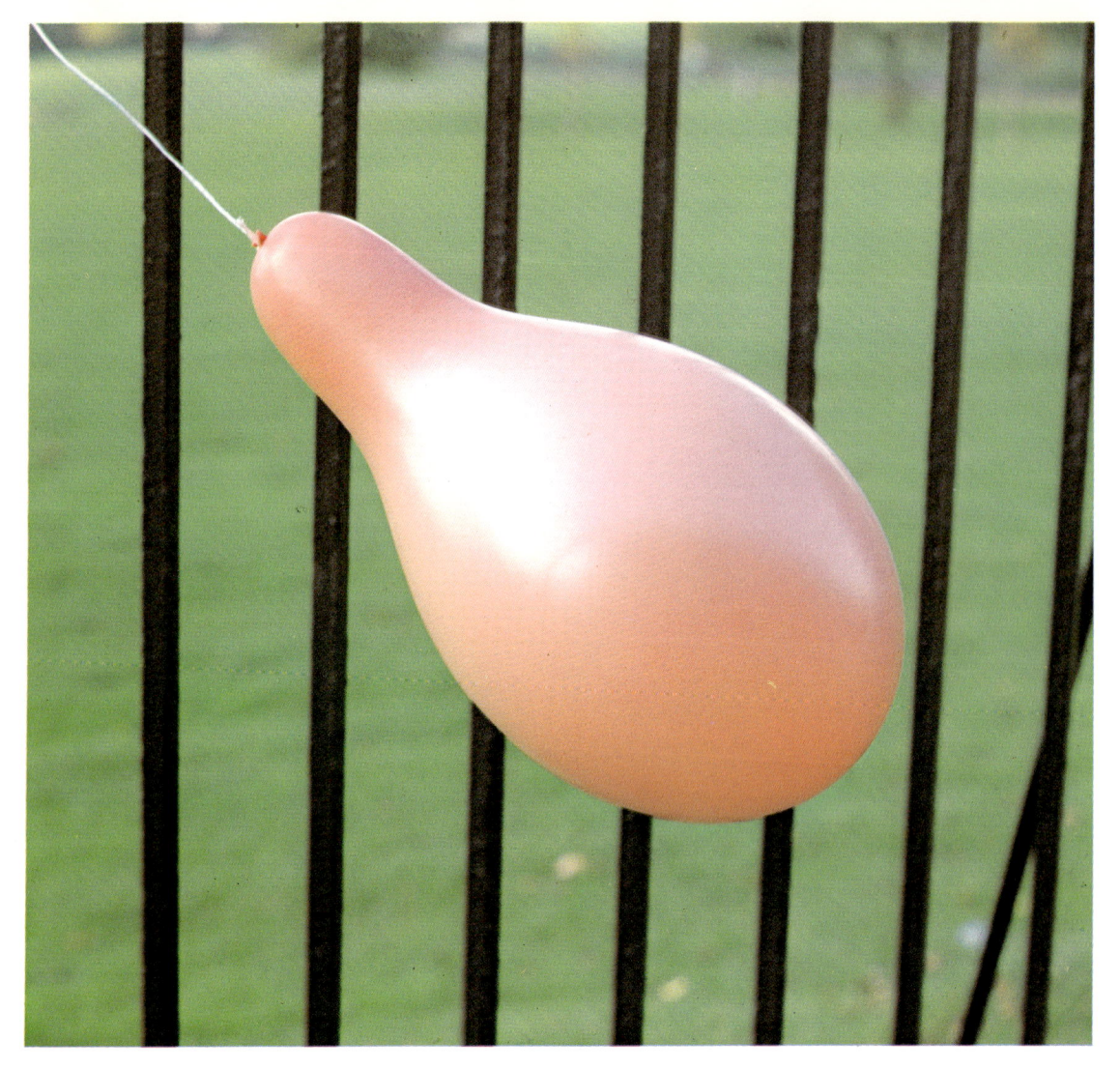

balloon

The children have balloons
at their party.

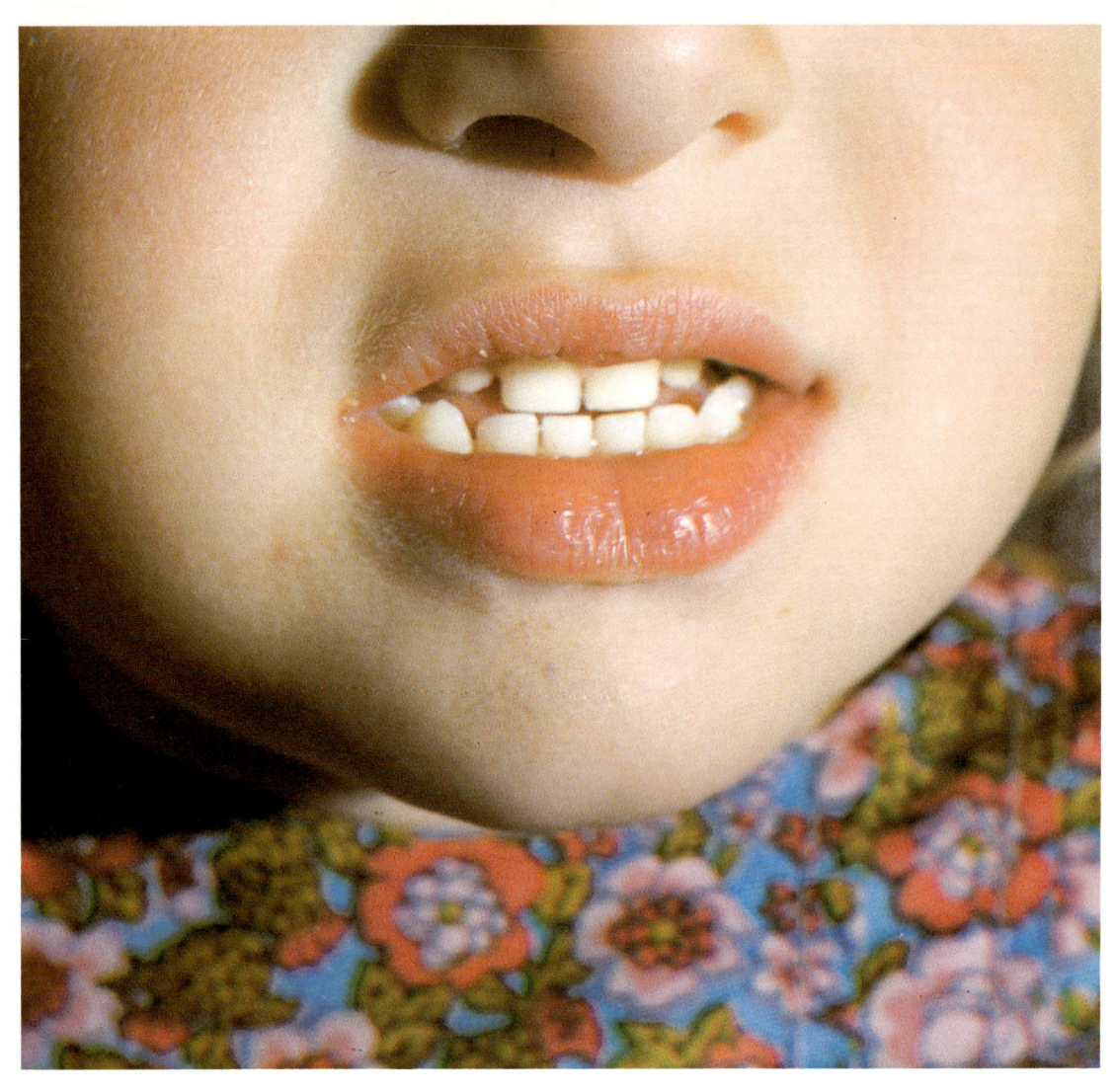

teeth

Jenny is cleaning her teeth.

bed

When Jenny is in bed,
Daddy reads her a story.

The Early Words Picture Book is based on research carried out at the University of Nottingham and Yale University into what children prefer to talk about when they start to speak. It accompanies the highly successful *First Words Picture Book*, by the same author, and introduces a further selection of the topics that occur most often in children's first words. Each topic is shown by itself and then 'in action' by superb colour photographs; all have a special fascination for children and provide a powerful stimulus to developing their language. Talking about the pictures with the child and asking questions, such as 'What is Jenny wearing? . . . What are the children doing? . . . What else do rabbits like to eat?' . . . all help to extend children's language as well as increasing their pleasure in a book that is based on what *children* are interested in.

Dr Bill Gillham is one of the UK's leading educational psychologists and an authority on early language development.

First published in 1983
by Methuen Children's Books Ltd
This Magnet edition first published in 1988
by Methuen Children's Books Ltd
11 New Fetter Lane, London EC4P 4EE
Text copyright © 1983 Bill Gillham
Illustrations copyright © 1983 Bill Gillham and Sam Grainger
Printed in Great Britain

ISBN 0 416 07472 3

This paperback is sold subject to the condition
that it shall not, by way of trade or otherwise,
be lent, re-sold, hired out or otherwise circulated
without the publisher's prior consent in any form
of binding or cover other than that in which
it is published and without a similar condition
including this condition being imposed
on the subsequent purchaser.